FOAL

DISCOVERING

STEM at the
Museum

STEM
▶ in the ◀
Real
World

Amy Hayes

PowerKiDS
press.

New York

Published in 2016 by The Rosen Publishing Group, Inc.
29 East 21st Street, New York, NY 10010

First Edition

Editor: Sarah Machajewski
Book Design: Mickey Harmon

Photo Credits: Cover (museum) mariakraynova/Shutterstock.com; cover, pp. 1, 3–4, 6, 8, 10, 12, 14, 16, 18, 20, 22–24 (banner design) linagifts/Shutterstock.com; cover, pp. 1, 4, 6, 14 (logo/caption box) Vjom/Shutterstock.com; p. 5 BestPhotoPlus/Shutterstock.com; p. 7 Kiev.Victor/Shutterstock.com; p. 9 Marcio Jose Bastos Silva/Shutterstock.com; p. 11 HANK MORGAN/Science Source/Getty Images; p. 13 NASA/Paul E. Alers/iStockphoto.com; p. 15 Steve Dunwell/Photolibrary/Getty Images; p. 17 (main) Hisham Ibrahim/Photodisc/Getty Images; p. 17 (inset) Alex Wong/Staff/Getty Images News/Getty Images; p. 19 SasinT/Shutterstock.com; p. 21 lapon pinta/Shutterstock.com; p. 22 Fuse/Thinkstock.com.

Library of Congress Cataloging-in-Publication Data

Hayes, Amy, author.
 Discovering STEM at the museum / Amy Hayes.
    pages cm. — (STEM in the real world)
 Includes bibliographical references and index.
 ISBN 978-1-4994-0919-2 (pbk.)
 ISBN 978-1-4994-0922-2 (6 pack)
 ISBN 978-1-4994-0969-7 (library binding)
 1. Museums—Juvenile literature. 2. Museums—Educational aspects—Juvenile literature. I. Title. II. Title: Discovering science, technology, engineering, and math at the museum.
 AM7.H39 2016
 069—dc23
                                    2014050043

Manufactured in the United States of America

CPSIA Compliance Information: Batch #WS15PK: For Further Information contact Rosen Publishing, New York, New York at 1-800-237-9932

Contents

What's a Museum?

Have you ever been to a museum? A museum is a place that collects and displays historical and artistic objects for people to see. You may have visited one on a school trip or maybe with your family on a weekend. Museums are great places to learn about our world.

Museums open their doors to lots of visitors every day. They use STEM to run smoothly. "STEM" stands for "science, **technology**, **engineering**, and math." Let's learn more about museums and how they use STEM!

A museum can teach you about science, history, art, and so much more!

Exciting Exhibits

Science museums collect objects that help people learn. They have **exhibits** on everything from spiders to electricity to outer space! Some museums even have animal bones or mummies on display. All these things are connected to science, which is the "S" in STEM.

Exhibits are special collections created by **experts** to teach visitors about a certain subject. Sometimes they're about a time period or a type of plant. Exhibits are a great way to learn about science, but they can teach us about technology, engineering, and math, too.

Exhibits can be anywhere in a science museum. They can be on the wall, in the middle of the room, or even hanging from the ceiling!

Paleontology and Bones

Some natural history museums have a really cool exhibit—dinosaur bones! There are many things to learn from them. The study of animal **fossils** is an important kind of science. It's called **paleontology**.

Paleontology can tell us a lot about what Earth was like millions of years ago. Sometimes bones from the same dinosaurs are found in different areas of the world! This means they lived when the **continents** were joined together as a huge landmass.

STEM Smarts

Some scientists work with fossils and bones. They study dinosaur remains to learn about what Earth was like when dinosaurs were alive.

A natural history museum is one that displays exhibits about subjects in the natural world, such as the remains of the dinosaur pictured here.

Museum Security

Art museums display beautiful art. Sometimes the art is very valuable or important. It can also be expensive. Museums have to keep the art and other things in their collections safe. To do this, they must use **security** technology.

The "T" in STEM stands for technology. Technology is used in every room of a museum, though you may not see it. Museums have security cameras and door alarms. There's also technology that senses movement and even heat sensors that keep exhibits safe.

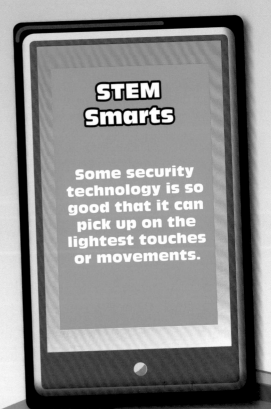

STEM Smarts

Some security technology is so good that it can pick up on the lightest touches or movements.

This is a security robot called the SR2. It travels from room to room in the Los Angeles County Museum of Art. How does it know where to go? Its computer has a built-in map of every room in the museum.

11

Tickets to the IMAX

Some museums show IMAX movies. The movies may be about the stars, life in the sea, or dinosaurs. IMAX movies are shown on huge screens, which are sometimes shaped like a **dome**.

A special kind of technology is used to make IMAX movies. The camera used to shoot the movie is very big and can weigh up to 240 pounds (109 kg)! Moviemakers also use a special **film** that's 10 times the size of usual film. This technology allows movies to fit properly on a huge screen.

STEM Smarts

Technology is a part of everyday life. When you turn on a TV, use a computer, or open an app, you're seeing technology at work.

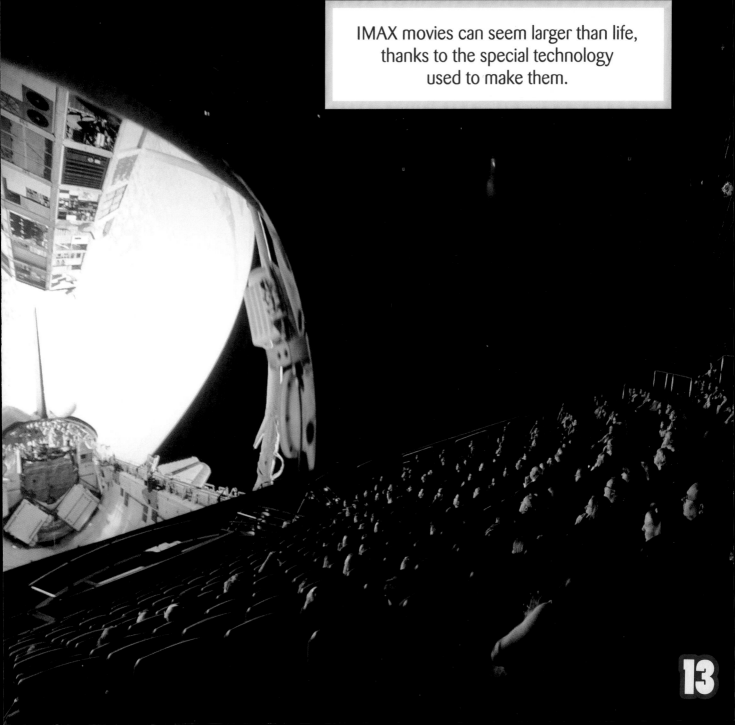

IMAX movies can seem larger than life,
thanks to the special technology
used to make them.

13

Flying High

Some museums have exhibits that help us understand what life was like in the past. They often show how STEM subjects have changed over time. Some of the coolest museums focus on the history of engineering, which is the "E" in STEM.

Museums such as the Smithsonian National Air and Space Museum in Washington, D.C., look at how people learned to make airplanes. Some museums have entire planes on display! Other museums show cars, motorcycles, lightbulbs, and even old ways of making glass. These exhibits teach visitors how engineering has shaped our world.

The Smithsonian National Air and Space Museum has exhibits ranging from the very first airplanes to the space shuttle *Discovery*.

STEM Smarts

Many history museums have exhibits about engineering because engineering has shaped our lives. Without engineering, we wouldn't have jet planes, robots, or even sports stadiums!

Protecting and Preserving

History museums display objects that are hundreds and even thousands of years old. They may have old kinds of paper, cloth, or tools people made and used long ago. These objects can be very delicate, which means they can break easily. Museums use technology and engineering, such as climate control, to keep **artifacts** from falling apart.

Climate control is when a space is engineered to be a certain **temperature** and **humidity**. Most artifacts need a cool, dry place. Climate control machines work to keep rooms and display cases at the right levels.

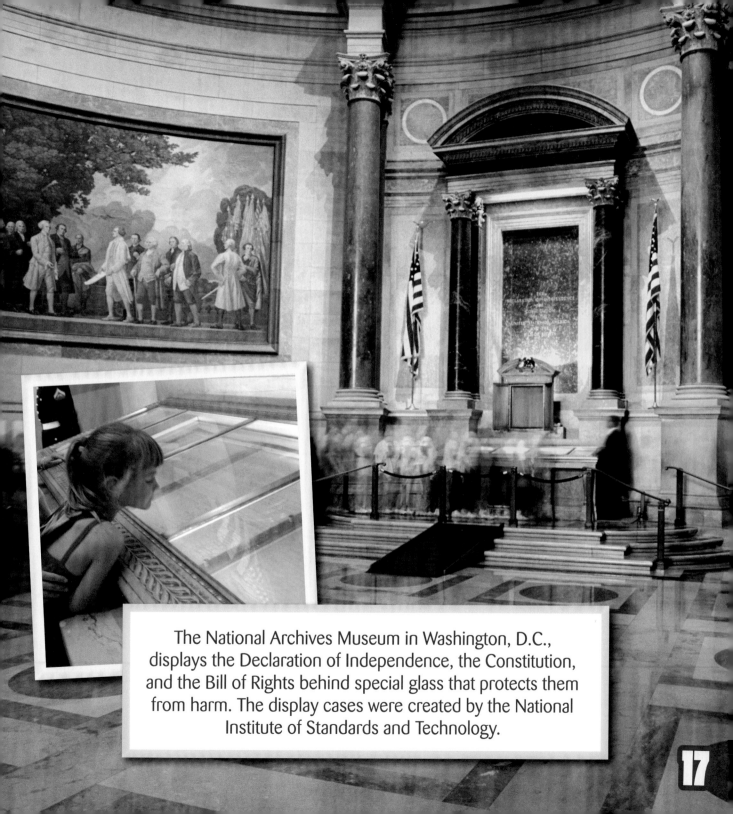

The National Archives Museum in Washington, D.C., displays the Declaration of Independence, the Constitution, and the Bill of Rights behind special glass that protects them from harm. The display cases were created by the National Institute of Standards and Technology.

Keeping Track of It All

Math, the "M" in STEM, is an important part of making sure a museum runs smoothly. Math helps museum workers keep track of all the inventory, or pieces in a museum's collection.

Museum workers use math to count the objects and make sure they're stored in the right places. They also use math to know if the museum has enough money to buy more pieces or if it has to sell pieces to make money.

STEM Smarts

Museums lend their pieces to other museums for special traveling exhibits. Math helps workers keep track of where exhibits are, even when they're around the world!

Sometimes a museum has so many objects that the extras are kept in a separate building. Taking inventory can be quite a challenge, but math makes it possible.

May I Have Your Ticket?

Math isn't just used for keeping track of inventory. It's also used to keep track of visitors. How many people come to the museum on a certain day? How many people saw a special exhibit? How much money did the museum earn in a week?

People in charge of the museum use ticket sales to learn how many people visit the museum every day. Tracking ticket sales lets the people in charge know how popular their exhibits are. It also helps the museum keep track of the money it earns.

Some museums are so popular that they have long lines and give out only so many tickets per hour. This is the line at the Louvre, a famous art museum in Paris.

Finding STEM on Your Own

Going to a museum can be a great way to learn about STEM in the world around you. It's also a lot of fun!

The next time you visit a museum, see if you can find STEM at work. Learn about science and try to find the traces of museum security. Look for an example of engineering, or feel the climate control. Think about the number of pieces in the museum, and try to keep your own inventory. STEM is all around you. Go out and find it!

Glossary

artifact: Something made by people in the past.

continent: One of Earth's seven great landmasses.

dome: A rounded roof of a building.

engineering: The use of science and math to improve our world.

exhibit: A public display at a museum.

expert: A person who has a lot of knowledge about a certain subject.

film: A thin strip of plastic used to record movies or pictures.

fossil: Hardened remains of a living thing that lived long ago.

humidity: The amount of water, in gas form, in the air.

paleontology: A branch of science that deals with animal and plant fossils.

security: Actions taken to keep something safe.

technology: The way people do something using tools. Also, the tools that they use.

temperature: How hot or cold something is.

Index

Websites

Due to the changing nature of Internet links, PowerKids Press has developed an online list of websites related to the subject of this book. This site is updated regularly. Please use this link to access the list: www.powerkidslinks.com/stem/muse